Chasing Petals in the Sun

Padmini Govender

ISBN 978-1-0492-3305-5 - Print

978-1-0492-3306-2 - eBook

Printed in the Republic of South Africa.

Copyright © Padmini Govender 2025

All rights reserved. No part of this book may be reproduced in any form or by any electronic or mechanical means, including information storage and retrieval systems, without written permission from the author, except in the case of a reviewer, who may quote brief passages embodied in critical articles or in a review. Trademarked names appear throughout this book. Rather than use a trademark symbol with every occurrence of a trademarked name, names are used in an editorial fashion, with no intention of infringement of the respective owner's trademark. The information in this book is distributed on an "as is" basis, without warranty. Although every precaution has been taken in the preparation of this work, neither the author nor the publisher shall have any liability to any person or entity with respect to any loss or damage caused or alleged to be caused directly or indirectly by the information contained in this book.

Dedication

Dedicated to my husband Sydney – always willing to travel, so that I can make my dreams come true. A wholesome companion, loving, patient and always adventurous. This is just one of many of our travel trips. The universe has opened the travel itineraries, and we choose where and when.

A photographic journey across the country.

Thousands of stunning pictures, and yet

the camera fails to do justice to the beauty

of our country and land.

What the heart and soul captured

is indescribable and inimitable.

My poetry shares some of the moments in words.

A longing to find a sense of ipseity.
That wild abandon not to care
of what is expected of me,
to remain unfettered by
what seems comfortable,
unburdened by societal dictates,
to be free from the shackles
of others imprisoned in shallowness.

A half-baked thought written down hastily,
just to get New Year's resolutions done.
Yet it was not some frivolous daydream.
My soul had longed for this for ages,
salivating over blogs and books to see the same.
A vision, a dream, an "I want this" manifested
into a road trip beyond expectations,
divinely orchestrated in my favour,
leaving my heart in awe and my soul satisfied.

Secrets between sisters, my soul wish.

This year, not another year,

was to go see the wildflowers. Full stop.

Me too, me too, we planned and plotted

for months, the excitement unending.

Wildflowers became chasing petals in the sun,

touching the freezing Atlantic Ocean,

driving the dry Karoo, food frenzies,

and late-night fireside chats.

All too soon, it became memories,

captured in our souls for reminiscing.

The city of gold fades in the distance.

A different kind of peace settles.

The open roads, farmland, barren land.

Darkness gives way to the faint rising sun.

The morning stars disappear till night.

Road trips take us to places

that bring us home to ourselves.

The moon standing in glory,

a blazing sun already high,

each cognizant of the other,

neither boastful nor abrasive.

Each retreats with grace

and resurfaces with tenderness.

Community, a meaningless word.
In this world we call home,
humans cannot exist in harmony,
not with ourselves, not with nature.
Each out to drown the other,
holding them under water
until there is no more breath.

Yet nature exists with unwritten rules,
each living as it is intended,
harming not out of rage and spite,
coexisting without imposing, simply being.

Open roads can be lonely

for empty minds and hearts.
Yes, for the eye that can see
beyond the tar stretching ahead,
there is the unfathomable beauty,
the natural wonders of the world,
a masterpiece on canvas,
each element carefully selected,
placed for maximum effect.
Cloudy skies, rising mountains,
rocks and flowers, gravel,
nothing that man can lay claim to.

Aukoerebis.

The Senqu in Lesotho,
Orange River in South Africa,
flowing seaward, cutting through country,
plunging into the Augrabies Falls.

A natural wonder of cataracts and rapids,
the water flows relentlessly, never gently.
The Khoi called it the "great noise,"
the "Aukoerebis."

Cascading flow plummeting
into the gorge below,
thundering through rocky formations,
gushing on, the journey continues.

Quite unlike the Smoke that Thunders,

yet the Augrabies National Falls holds its own.

Water cascading mightily into the gorge below,

in the silence, all you hear is the crash and splash.

The walk about the Falls is breathtaking.

To think that at one point, the water was at this level,

and over centuries, nature remoulds the area.

Dassies stare at us in wonder, a constant distraction;

we stare back, as we walk away, still in awe.

The Kokerboom, or quiver trees.

No, they do not quiver in fear of the thunderous roar
of the Orange River as it plummets into the gorge.
They stand tall and strong at Augrabies Falls,
giant aloes with a distinctive silhouette.
The Khoisan once used the branches to make quivers,
hence the name of the trees so majestic.
A tree hugger by nature, the tree returned the love.

Eyes searching beauty,
expectations of grandeur,
breathtaking first bloom.

       A handful of wildflowers wilting,
          waiting for the morning sun,
          the warmth unfurling the petals
          for a magnanimous show of colour.

Springbok, small-town charm,

with a whole lot of heart

and wildflowers, masses of them.

Quaint little houses, soft people,

the colours run riot on the kerbs,

streetsides, along the roads.

Hands long to cut a bunch for a vase,

heart says no, leave them be,

far more beautiful naturally outdoors.

The Moon, it follows me, I tell you,
always around, whether whole or not,
shining its light and love wherever I may be.
It feels like home when I glance up
to see its radiant face, or just the sliver.

Golden colour, as warm as the sun itself,
seeking the gentle splash of rain
to awaken the once-dormant seeds
that flourish into a field of wildflowers.
A sight that only the soul can feel;
the eye may see, but the heart will hold.
Once-parched Namaqualand, it comes alive
in a flurry of colour twirling in the wind.

Wildflowers are defiant little souls,

pushing through gravel and stone,

blooming, blossoming, without care.

Alone, we are stronger on our own.

The midmorning sun slowly warms the earth.
The veld comes alive, almost magically,
a palette of colour, a masterpiece.
Nature puts on a show for only a short while.
The wildflowers, the stars that beckon
the hearts of many from across the world.
The camera clicks for posterity,
the heart and soul for eternity.
These beauties are mesmerizing.
As the sun moves towards the horizon,
the flowers go back to sleep for the night.
Blink, and one can miss them dancing
in the breeze under the morning sun.

The universe conspires to conjure

magical moments that restore a soul.

The morning sun rising languidly,

the dance of colour on the horizon.

As the sun dips low, kissing the moon,

the stars twinkle almost coyly.

The river rushes seaward,
flowing down to Die Mond,
a tiny hamlet, Alexander Bay,
dilapidated and seemingly forgotten,
but for the mining operation.
Standing at the mouth of the river,
as it spews forth into the ocean,
South Africa waving to Namibia,
the Orange River dividing the land.

The white sand stretches,

bare and barren little towns.

Is this it? This life?

People sitting about, busy,

busy with nothing,

for there is nothing to do,

nothing to boost the lives

of people who seem to be forgotten

on the edge of South Africa.

Wild horses crisscrossing the roads

and the fields, without care or concern,

free to be, without decorum,

like thoughts that flow in silence.

They move with grace, without fear,

for there are no fences to rein them in.

Soft rain against the gloomy skies,

the sea, sad and forlorn, lonely.

Seaweed and kelp strewn about,

fishing boats on the restless sea.

Fishermen agitated on the shore,

for the ocean is their home.

Mountains rise like kings,

shadows as the sun shines,

Cederberg beauty.

The Protea - South Africa's national flower,
natural beauty in various shades and shapes,
growing in the wild, without nurturing,
standing tall, gracefully amongst the rocks.

The ritual of dance,

ancient and sacred,

to the music of silence.

What can't be heard,

the heart and soul will hear.

In the stillness of the Cederberg mountains,
I feel my soul breathe, quietly and in peace.
The night is cold, but brings a tranquil rest,
undisturbed and deep, awakening to the sun.
Long walks in the warm sun, carpet of colour,
varying hues and shades, undefined scent,
heady with the multi-species of wildflowers.
The sun sets low, the wind startling the trees.
As night falls, the sky becomes a riot of light,
the stars dancing in the darkness, twinkling
to an orchestra playing in the universe.

In the shadows of the mountains,

the orchards dance in the breeze,

a flourish of leaves and fruit.

The cool early spring chill,

the warmth of the log fire.

Night brings a quiet silence,

restorative therapy for the soul.

Chanoyu, the gentle art of a tea ceremony.

Glass teapot standing over the burner,

tea brewing without hurry, a fusion of flavour.

Thoughts amble by, aimlessly, unfettered,

the empty seat beckoning at a table

beneath the oak tree in the garden.

Sipping tea slowly, the gentle art of life.

The tree bare, against the blue sky,

mountains jeering from the distance.

It doesn't shudder at itself in disgust,

nor does it shy away from sight.

It stands tall, roots deeply grounded,

majestically waiting for its season

when it is dressed in foliage and flowers.

Agterbaai.

St Helena Bay, "Agterbaai," the locals call it.
The rocky seabed, strewn with shipwrecks,
many a story remains untold
of sailors lurking in the wrecks,
searching for a way out from
the depths of their ocean graves.

The local fishermen will tell tales
of the big catches - their livelihood,
and of the things that lurk in the water,
of why they don't go out alone,
and why they hear the clanging
in the dead of the night when they sleep,
or why the wind wails for days on end.

Sand curves away from the whitewashed walls

towards the rock and icy Atlantic.

Oystercatchers scurry about frantically,

picking at ghost crabs and mussels.

Terns and seagulls dip into the sea,

gracefully coming away with a morsel.

The seashore strewn with seashells,

the white sand soft under my feet.

There are no waves crashing on the shoreline.
The ocean rocks itself gently, there by Langebaan.
The blue-green water, idyllic and island-like.
Time stands still, gazing across the bay,
wondering about die strandloper and his life
as he manoeuvred through the lagoon,
without disturbing the natural wonders,
leaving only footprints as he trekked.

Hurtling across the sand,

the ocean calling one home,

seagulls diving low.

        The roving singer,

           strumming a beat-up guitar,

              singing from the heart.

The ocean beckons gently over the grassy dunes,

the whitewashed walls obscuring the beauty

from the prying eyes of unwanted strangers.

Oystercatchers rush frantically on the shoreline,

dancing in the waves, picking at the morsels washed ashore.

Boats rocking to the lullaby of the ocean,

no waves, just a rhythmic lull of the water.

On the pristine white sand, soft and warm,

the sky mesmerized with its own reflection.

The mist rises slowly

over a city coming alive.

Bo-Kaap throwing colour

on the view below.

A city that is magical

for those who can afford

the beauty it displays:

the rich, the digital nomads,

the constant stream of visitors,

hypnotised by the glamour of it all.

A working trap, a drug den

for those who live on the fringes.

The vineyards hold a certain old charm,
like old money, rich wealth passed down.
The vines are still sleeping, though,
the harvests from prior years
already bottled or infusing in barrels.
Soon the last cooler days of late winter
or early spring will dissipate,
and the vines will sprout again,
lush foliage, beautiful vines,
a promise for the future.
Wine, like all good things in life,
takes time, effort, and patience.

The lone surfer,

trying to catch the waves,

practicing with passion

before the crowds come.

The water remains icy,

yet he is fixated to remain

standing upright on the board.

The ocean tries to throw him off.

Determination and discipline:

core to success in life, in any area.

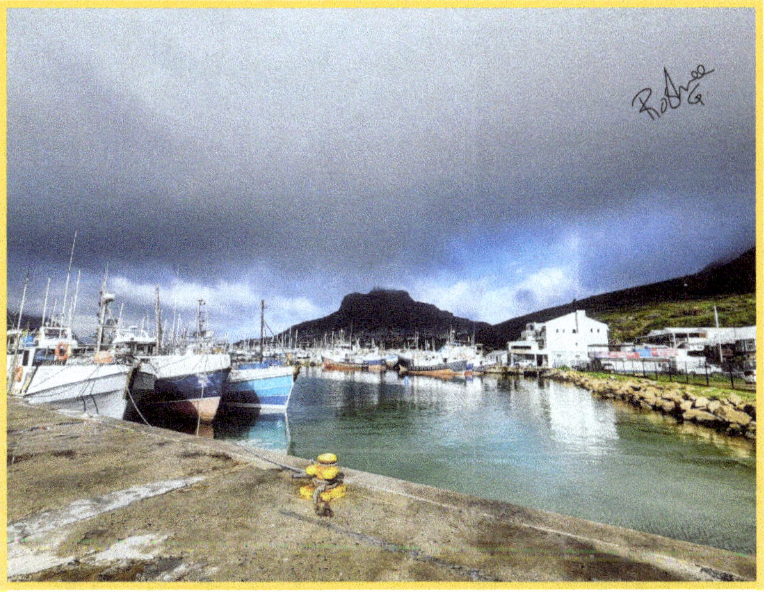

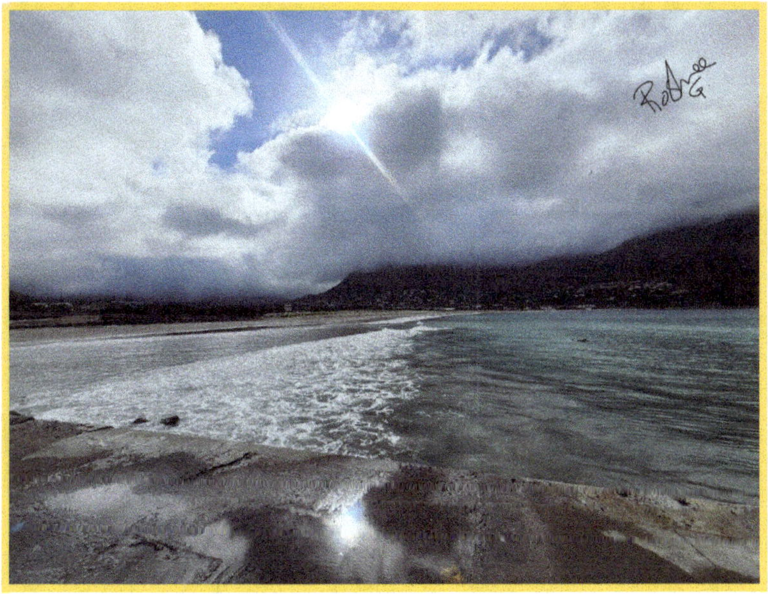

A midday sun, high in the sky,
its aura extending like a rainbow.
What is this phenomenon?
A magical moment in those few minutes,
the universe throwing surprises
as we wander along back home.

The Big Hole still holds interest.
Visitors pour into the now museum-style mine,
largely lucrative mining since about 1875,
where thousands of migrant labourers
lost their lives to enrich the owners.
Today the mine stands as a monument,
yet the rest of Kimberley does not shine
like the wealth dragged from its belly,
monies meant for infrastructure,
feeding the bellies of the greedy instead.

Ek trek nie met ossewa nie,

maar met my hart en siel.

Nooit kan ek vergeet hoe

die land aan my gepraat het,

lewendig en dankbaar.

Hierdie land van ons is pragtig.

Travel feeds one's mind,

traipsing across the country,

heart and soul travel.

Getting to the tail end of a long road trip,

not with sadness, but gratitude.

Travel is good for the soul.

Bringing clarity to a life

otherwise run by the clock:

schedules and calendars.

Time and day seem irrelevant;

it is what it is, whenever.

Less is more - make a plan.

Living out of a suitcase is not for everyone.

It is different from opening full cupboards

"with nothing to wear."

A soft travel companion,

long chats, more desires shared with the universe.

Sleeps that are so restorative.

Small-town people with big hearts.

Oranges and nartjies left on the stoep,

no cost, no "enjoy that"

it's from the farm.

My other life seems so distant.
Everything that touched my soul
could not be caught on camera.
Some things were for my soul only.

Yes, we cannot be on holiday every day,
but every day we can do something small
to bring joy, whether it's a thing
like having coffee together,
sipping it slowly, watching the morning unfurl,
or a walk in the garden, feeling the earth,
smelling the roses,
or that late-night sneaky piece of chocolate.
I want my life to be a holiday every day;
that is my firm soul desire.

My heart saw more than my eyes did,

my soul felt the country as we travelled.

A restorative and soul-satisfying trip.

Travel does that. It awakens the dormant soul,

bringing to life the craving for life,

like the rain to the wildflowers.

Travel brings fresh perspective to the mundane.

Been to places and seen things

that my heart still cannot believe.

In my dream, I am seeing what still needs to be seen.

My soul is in awe of the beauty of our land.

A balm for a weary soul.

Travel soothes the soul,

bringing clarity to life.

New people, new places,

a life somewhere different.

The reality is our lives are

tied to the job and the clock.

Travel is that tiny distraction

in an otherwise mundane world.

Education may come out of books,

but travel educates the mind differently.

Learn more about oneself

and travel companions

than a thousand chats will reveal.

The little habits that are troublesome,

or the easy, affable personality.

Travel resets the soul to that which matters.

In the stillness of the waking hours,
pausing for a moment to breathe,
my soul overwhelmed with gratitude.
No ringing bells to awaken my heart,
just the silent music of the universe.

Is my soul restless again, I wonder,
gazing at the horizon with love.
Evocative dreams of places yet unseen,
lucidity endearing my heart to move.
Unfinished travel that must be done,
open spaces calling me fervently,
for that is where I am home.
What is it that has stirred a new awakening
deep in my soul for a passion-filled life?

Appeared in South Coast Herald Online

I am all that this land is,
what it was, and what it could be.
South Africa is my home.

Heritage so unique that it holds visitors in awe,
a melting pot of cultural differences,
essentially the same flowing through.
We fight to keep our identity individual,
yet take on the world to hold up our people.

I am of Indian descent, fourth generation,
but South African in every way.
Born and raised in the dusty streets of apartheid,
to a country being ripped apart by poverty,
crime and social injustice.
Yet this is home, a familiar comfort in the chaos that reigns.

We brought the iphuthu from the sugar mill compounds
into our homes; kremelpap in the suburbs.
We've taken the curry and atchar
from Durban to the streets in the townships.
We all search for the perfect chicken dust
and shisanyama on a Saturday afternoon.
Call it a lekker braai if you must.

Colour may separate us; sports unite us.
Food is the thread that holds it together.
Yet quintessentially, that thing of being South African
is simply being South African.

This is home. Yes, my roots touch the shores
of India, but this is where my soul belongs.
My every breath is South African.
It's just a vibe, a feeling.

This is home. Yes, my roots touch the shores
of India, but this is where my soul belongs.
My every breath is South African.
It's just a vibe, a feeling.

About the Author

Padmini Govender is a poet with a background in financial accounting, but words have always been her true calling. *Chasing Petals in the Sun* is her second collection, following her debut, *The Moon Child*.

This collection includes photographs she took during a road trip across beautiful South Africa, paired with short poetic reflections inspired by the landscapes and moments she encountered along the way. Her poetry is rooted in honesty and emotional depth, yet it consistently returns to peace. Through gentle imagery, mindful pauses, and quiet clarity, her work invites readers into spaces where the heart can soften and the spirit can breathe.

Over time, Padmini has strengthened her connection with mind, body, spirit, and soul, often turning to nature for grounding and clarity. Her poems reflect this path and the gentle resilience that comes with it. Her work has appeared in the South Coast Herald, Sakura Magazine, and Paper Trail Literary Journal. She has also contributed to the *Poetry is not Dead* anthology and to *Not Water, Just Ice* by Brett "Fish" Anderson.

Padmini Govender

www.ingramcontent.com/pod-product-compliance
Lightning Source LLC
LaVergne TN
LVHW020116080426
835507LV00042B/1903